ColoringFAITH

PUMPKIN SPICE & EVERYTHING NICE

COLORING BOOK

Illustrated by Julianne St. Clair

T0045773

HOW GRATEFUL AND THANKFUL

I am to the *Lord*

because he is so good.

I will SING praise

to the name of the Lord

WHO IS ABOVE

all *lords.*

PSALM 7:17 TLB

PUMPKIN
kisses &
HARVEST
WISHES

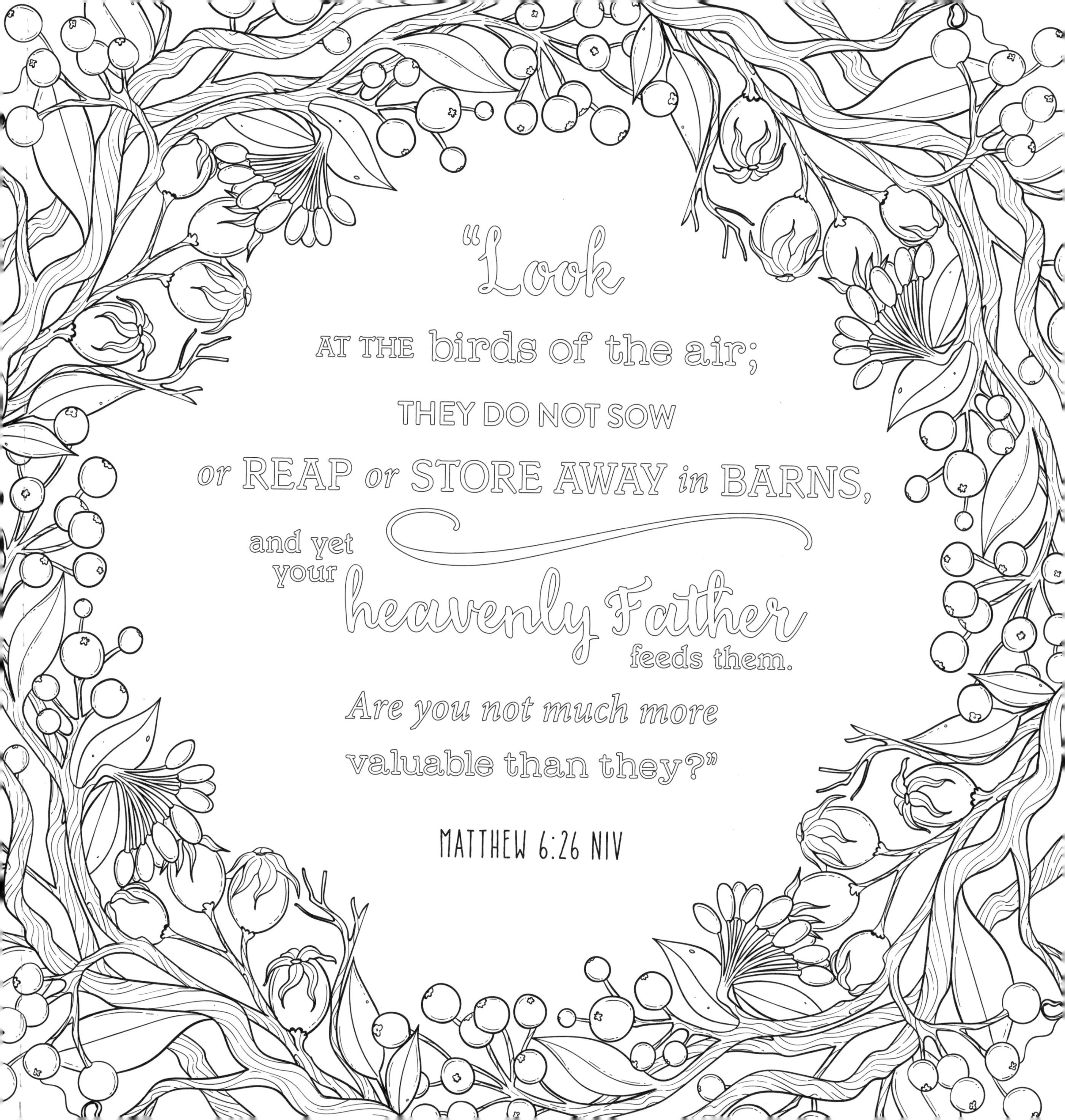

"Look at the birds of the air; they do not sow or reap or store away in barns, and yet your heavenly Father feeds them. Are you not much more valuable than they?"

MATTHEW 6:26 NIV

Autumn...
the YEAR'S LAST,
loveliest smile.
WILLIAM CULLEN BRYANT

O LORD our God,
all this abundance
that we have prepared
to build You a house
for Your holy name,
is from Your HAND,
and is all Your own.

1 CHRONICLES 29:16

PICK
of the
PATCH

AUTUMN

is the mellower season,

AND

what WE lose

IN *flowers*

we more than gain

IN *fruits.*

SAMUEL BUTLER

Pumpkin
SPICE
&
Everything
NICE

HOW
ABUNDANT
are the
good THINGS
&
that you have stored up
for those who
FEAR YOU.
PSALM 31:19 NIV

BE KIND.
BE thoughtful.
BE GENUINE.
but most of all, BE
thankful

LET US
not
BECOME WEARY IN DOING GOOD,
for at the proper time
WE WILL REAP
a HARVEST
if we DO NOT give up.
GALATIANS 6:9 NIV

LEAVES
are falling
AUTUMN
is calling

My God
shall SUPPLY ALL YOUR need
according to his riches
IN GLORY BY
Christ Jesus.
PHILIPPIANS 4:19

colored leaves

SWEATERS

scarves

hot chocolate

bonfires

BOOTS

crisp air
PUMPKIN EVERYTHING
CORN MAZES
HAYRIDES
CUDDLING UNDER BLANKETS

Oh, HOW GREAT is Your goodness...
WHICH YOU HAVE prepared for those who TRUST in You.
PSALM 31:19

Hoodies.
BONFIRES.
Cuddling.
Fall is here.

THIS
is the day the LORD
HAS MADE;
We will rejoice
AND BE
GLAD
in it.
PSALM 118:24

Hayrides
and
pumpkin pies
and
golden
SKIES

Oh,
give thanks to
THE LORD,
FOR HE IS good!
For His mercy
ENDURES
forever.
1 CHRONICLES 16:34

No spring nor summer
beauty hath such grace
as I have seen in
one autumnal face.
John Donne

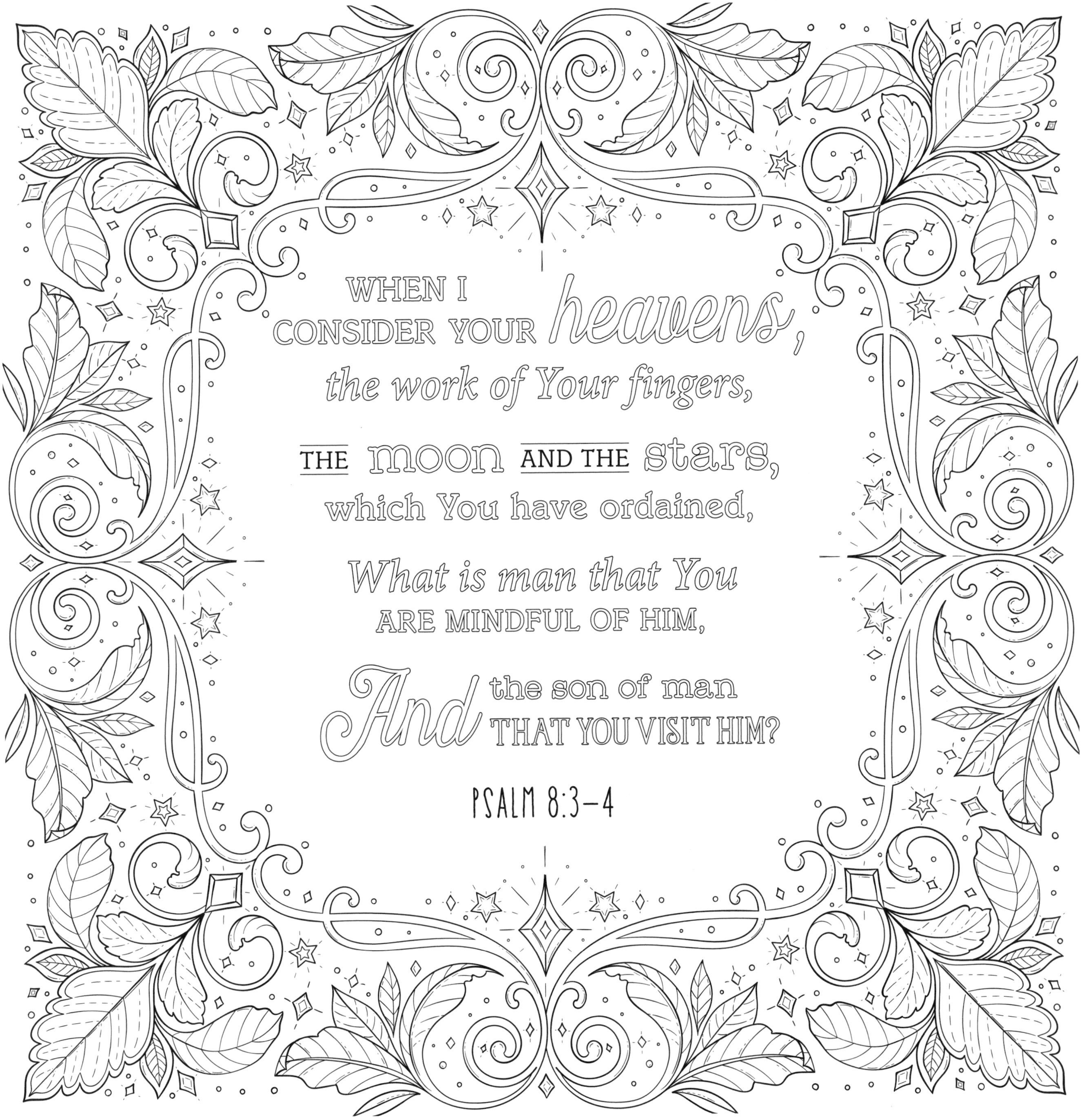
WHEN I CONSIDER YOUR heavens,
the work of Your fingers,
THE moon AND THE stars,
which You have ordained,
What is man that You
ARE MINDFUL OF HIM,
And the son of man
THAT YOU VISIT HIM?
PSALM 8:3–4

It's
Fall
Y'ALL

"As LONG as
the earth endures,
SEEDTIME and HARVEST,
COLD and HEAT,
SUMMER and WINTER,
DAY and NIGHT
will NEVER cease."
GENESIS 8:22 NIV

Every LEAF
speaks bliss to me,
fluttering from
the
AUTUMN tree.
EMILY BRONTË

PUMPKIN PATCH

THE EARTH
is THE LORD'S,
and all its fullness,
THE world
& those who dwell
THEREIN.
PSALM 24:1

Thankful
and
BLESSED

THE
heavens
declare THE GLORY of God;
THE skies
PROCLAIM the work of
HIS HANDS.
PSALM 19:1 NIV

Fall
IS IN THE
AIR

BE patient, then, brothers & sisters, until THE LORD'S coming. SEE how the farmer waits for the LAND to yield its valuable crop, patiently waiting for the AUTUMN and SPRING rains. YOU too, be patient and stand firm, because the Lord's coming is near.

JAMES 5:7–8 NIV

pumpkin pie
HOT COCOA
candy corn
CRISP APPLES
pumpkin spice
APPLE CIDER
FALL TREATS

THE
tints of
AUTUMN...
a mighty flower garden
BLOSSOMING under the SPELL
of the enchanter,
frost.
JOHN GREENLEAF WHITTIER

PUMPKIN
Spice
EVERYTHING!

I will PRAISE you,
LORD MY
God, with
all MY HEART;
I WILL glorify
YOUR name
FOREVER
— Psalm 86:12 —

I'm so glad
I LIVE IN
a world
WHERE THERE ARE
OCTOBERS.

L. M. MONTGOMERY,
ANNE OF GREEN GABLES

LET
us come before
His presence
WITH
THANKSGIVING.
PSALM 95:2

DELICIOUS
autumn!
MY VERY SOUL IS WEDDED TO IT,
and if I were a bird,
I would FLY about the EARTH
SEEKING THE SUCCESSIVE
AUTUMNS.
GEORGE ELIOT

I CANNOT *endure* to waste anything so PRECIOUS *as* *autumnal sunshine* *by staying* IN THE HOUSE. So I have *spent* *almost all* THE DAYLIGHT HOURS IN THE *open air.*

NATHANIEL HAWTHORNE

WAIT FOR the LORD, and He will come and Save YOU! BE BRAVE, stouthearted, & courageous. YES, WAIT and HE WILL HELP YOU.

— Psalm 27:14 TLB —

LET THE
peace
OF
GOD
RULE IN YOUR
hearts
AND BE
thankful

Colossians 3:15

HOW
beautifully
LEAVES GROW OLD.
HOW FULL OF
light and color
are their
LAST DAYS.
JOHN BURROUGHS

Just
BEFORE
THE death of flowers,
and BEFORE they
are buried in snow,
there comes a
festival season
when nature is all
aglow.

I WILL GIVE
THANKS to
YOU,
LORD,
with all my heart;
I WILL TELL OF
all your WONDERFUL
deeds.
PSALM 9:1 NIV

Thou blossom bright with autumn dew, and COLORED WITH THE heaven's own blue.
WILLIAM CULLEN BRYANT

WILD is the music of AUTUMNAL WINDS amongst the faded WOODS.
WILLIAM WORDSWORTH

Light BREEZE,
colorful LEAVES,
BARE trees.
It must be
autumn.

To EVERYTHING there
IS A season,
A TIME FOR EVERY
purpose under
heaven.
ECCLESIASTES 3:1